Anteaters

Anteaters

Sandra Lee

THE CHILD'S WORLD®, INC.

Copyright © 1999 by The Child's World®, Inc.
All rights reserved. No part of this book may be
reproduced or utilized in any form or by any means
without written permission from the publisher.
Printed in the United States of America.

Library of Congress Cataloging-in-Publication Data
Lee, Sandra.
Anteaters / by Sandra Lee.
p.   cm.
Includes index.
Summary: Describes the physical characteristics,
habits, and natural environment of the giant anteater
which makes its home in the swamps and open grasslands
of Central and South America.
ISBN 1-56766-498-9 (lib. bdg. : alk paper)
1. Myrmecophagidae—Juvenile literature.
[1. Anteaters.]   I. Title.
QL737.E24L44   1998
599.3'14—dc21   97-48259
CIP
AC

Photo Credits

© Alan & Sandy Carey: 19
© Francois Gohier, The National Audubon Society Collection/PR: 10, 24, 26
© Jany Sauvanet, The National Audubon Society Collection/PR: 29
© Jerry L. Ferrara, The National Audubon Society Collection/PR: 23
© Joe McDonald: 2
© 1994 Michele Burgess: 15
© Paul Crum, The National Audubon Society Collection/PR: 20
© Stan Wayman, The National Audubon Society Collection/PR: 13
© Ted Cheeseman: cover, 9, 30
© Walt Anderson: 6, 16

On the cover...

Front cover: This *giant anteater* is walking through some tall grass in Brazil.
Page 2: Giant anteaters like this one are very large.

Table of Contents

Imagine that you are walking across a grassland in South America. As you look over the land, you notice a large animal moving slowly through the tall grass. As it moves, it sniffs the ground with its long nose. What could this strange creature be? It's an anteater!

⇐ This giant anteater is walking on a Brazilian grassland.

Where Do Anteaters Live?

Anteaters live only in Central and South America. Some live in wet, swampy areas. Others live on huge grasslands. And some make their homes in thick, green forests.

This *northern tamandua anteater* is searching in the grass for food. ⇒

Anteaters live in areas where they can find their favorite foods—ants, termites, grubs, and caterpillars. In Central and South America, these insects are everywhere—especially in the jungles and grasslands.

Are There Different Kinds of Anteaters?

There are three different kinds of anteaters. *Silky anteaters* are small and have soft, silky fur. *Tamandua* (tuh–MAN–duh–wuh) *anteaters* are a little bigger. They have short, thick hair all over their bodies. *Giant anteaters* are the most common type. They are very large. They also look the strangest.

It is easy to see how thick this tamandua anteater's fur is. ⇒

What Do Anteaters Look Like?

Anteaters are known for their long, tubelike **muzzles**, or mouths. The opening at the end of the muzzle is only big enough for the anteater's long, sticky tongue to go in and out. The tongue is so long, it can lick things two feet away!

These giant anteaters live in a zoo. ⇒

Most anteaters are covered with coarse, stiff hair that is brown or gray. They have wide, bushy tails and big, strong legs with sharp claws. Most anteaters have black and white stripes on their bodies, too. This coloring helps the anteaters hide. Coloring that helps an animal hide is called **camouflage**.

How Do Anteaters Eat?

Anteaters have a powerful sense of smell. As they move along, they sniff everywhere to find food. When they find an ant or termite nest, they start to dig. Their strong legs and sharp claws soon tear a hole in the nest. The hole is usually only big enough for the anteater to put its muzzle inside. As the ants or termites try to escape, the anteater flicks its long tongue in and out. The insects get caught on the tongue's sticky surface and are quickly brought to the anteater's mouth.

This tamandua anteater has found an ant's nest in a tree. ⇒

Anteaters do not have any teeth. So how do they chew? Instead of chewing, they smash their food against the sides and roofs of their mouths.

It takes a lot of food to fill up an anteater. In fact, one anteater can eat over 35,000 ants or termites in one day! Even though anteaters can eat a lot, they are very careful to save their source of food. They never destroy an ant or termite nest. After eating some bugs from one nest, the anteater moves on to find another. That way, there will always be food for the anteater to find.

⇐ This *black anteater* is eating termites.

What Are Baby Anteaters Like?

Anteaters are **solitary** animals, which means that they like to live alone. The only time anteaters get together is to mate. Six months after a male and female anteater mate, one baby is born. Right after birth, the baby anteater climbs onto its mother's back. It wiggles and climbs until it is completely hidden in its mother's fur. There the baby is safe. Its markings make it look like just another part of the mother's back. The baby hangs on tightly. If it falls off the mother's back, it makes short, shrill whistling sounds.

This young giant anteater is safe while it rides on its mother's back. ⇒

Anteaters belong to a group of animals called **mammals**. Mammals have hair all over their bodies and feed their babies milk from their bodies. Cows and people are mammals, too. Until it is about six months old, the baby anteater drinks its mother's milk. When the baby is old enough, the mother teaches it how to eat other foods.

Over time, the baby anteater learns to take short, careful trips away from its mother's back. When it is tired or frightened, the baby quickly climbs onto its mother's back again. As the baby grows, it becomes a heavy load for the mother. She must walk slowly and carefully. Sometimes mother anteaters with big babies look clumsy!

The young anteater stays with its mother until it is about two years old. Then it is finally ready to live on its own.

Do Anteaters Have Enemies?

Anteaters do not have many enemies. Sometimes jungle cats such as *pumas* or *jaguars* hunt anteaters for food. But the anteater's most dangerous enemy is people. Every day, some of the forests and grasslands where anteaters live are being destroyed. Without a place to live and food to eat, anteaters could be in danger of dying out someday.

Silky anteaters like this one need thick forests in which to live. ⇒

Anteaters are strange-looking creatures. But without them, the forests and grasslands of South America would have too many ants and termites. So the next time you think something looks strange, think about the anteater. The weird way something looks might just be the very thing that makes it special!

⇐ This giant anteater is searching for food in some tall grass.

Glossary

camouflage (KA–moo–flazh)
Camouflage is coloring that helps an animal blend in with its surroundings. An anteater's stripes act as camouflage.

mammals (MA–mullz)
Mammals are animals that have hair all over their bodies and feed their babies milk from their bodies. Cows, people, and anteaters are all mammals.

muzzle (MUH–zull)
A muzzle is an anteater's long mouth. The only thing that fits through an anteater's muzzle is its long, sticky tongue.

solitary (SAH–lih–tare–ee)
A solitary animal likes to live alone. Anteaters are solitary animals.

Index